CAERLEON

'Scenes Saved'
How We Were - How We Are

by Norman Stevens

Foreword by
Canon Arthur Edwards
Vicar of Caerleon with Llanhennock

Old Bakehouse Publications

Abertillery

© Norman Stevens

First published in October 2007

The rights of the author to this work has
been asserted by him in accordance with the Copyright,
Designs and Patents Act, 1993.

ISBN 978-1-905967-04-9

Published in the U.K. by
Old Bakehouse Publications
Church Street,
Abertillery, Gwent NP13 1EA
Telephone: 01495 212600 Fax: 01495 216222
E-mail: theoldbakeprint@btconnect.com
Website: www.oldbakehouseprint.co.uk

Made and printed in the UK
by J.R. Davies (Printers) Ltd.

British Library Cataloguing in Publication Data: a catalogue
record for this book is available from the British Library.

Foreword
by Canon Arthur Edwards
Vicar of Caerleon with Llanhennock

It's a privilege and a pleasure to be asked to introduce the fourth in this excellent series of photographs of Caerleon by Norman Stevens who has become an institution in his own right here and needs no introduction from me. He himself has thanked the many people who have contributed to this rich assortment of treasures that will provide such a valuable quarry of evidence for the social historian who must one day write the history of Caerleon, perhaps at our local University.

In the meantime it's good to have these reminders of the great and the good in our community, including two who received M.B.E.s in recent honours lists as well as three of my distinguished predecessors in the twentieth century who, between them, served the parish and people of Caerleon for sixty years. It's good to have photographs recording the retirements of David and Carol Jones from the post office and Mrs. Richards from the garage. We wish them all happy retirements and recall also with some sadness the photographs of others who made good contributions to our corporate life but whose funerals I have conducted in recent years. For the fun and the friendships recorded here, thank you, Norman.

Arthur Edwards

Shown right:
A commemorative dish to
celebrate 1900 years of Caerleon
as a centre of population
AD75 to 1975.

Introduction

Greetings to all. Once again I have the pleasure to have embarked on a project to record the past scenes of Caerleon life and material changes, from fashions in clothing, motor vehicles, buildings and people. All of these are designed to show the various eras of time and the new interests and economic changes that have affected our choice of living, working conditions and social interests.

All the material that has been used to do this has been the result of generous helpful interest by present residents, former residents and friends of Caerleon. All freely offered as an expression of goodwill to preserve the culture and memories of life and personalities that have been and will be an enduring contribution of the past and a significant reminder to the future generations of the lessons, good decisions and sometimes not so good! that have shaped our lives and environment.

It is highly probable that more photographs and ephemera of days past are lurking in shoe boxes or albums, that if not recorded, together with the family names and remembrances will ultimately vanish into the proverbial black bag.

Please make the effort. I do not remove any items from your possession but can copy photographs at your own home by arrangement.

Once, again my sincere thanks for your interest, comments and co-operation which literally without which this book could not have been completed.

Norman Stevens

Please contact me
  11 Home Farm Close, Caerleon, Gwent NP18 3SH   Tel: 01633 420187

Dedicated to
NICK CARTER
Lieutenant Commander, M.V.O. Royal Navy Rtd.
'Member of the Royal Victorian Order'
Former Keeper and Steward of the Royal Apartments
The Royal Yacht Britannia
my friend and colleague of many years who was cruelly deprived
by illness from a well earned retirement after a most distinguished
and successful career
May 1936 - January 2001

Caerleon

Contents

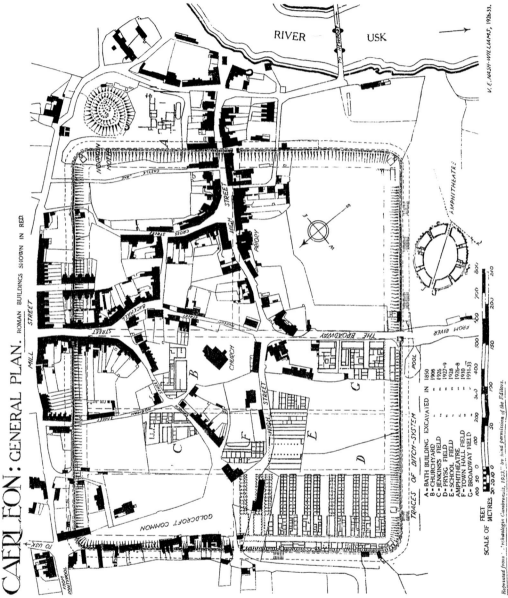

A 1933 Caerleon Town Plan with the darkened areas superimposed as an overlay on the Roman Fortress of Isca in AD 150.

6

Etchings of Caerleon circa. 1790

An etching dating from about 1790 and where the bushes are seen on the left is approximately where the stone-built bridge of 1805/1810 spanned the River Usk. The substantial house stands close to the corner of the field by the side of White Hart Lane whilst The Hanbury Arms would be appearing further to the right.

7

Etchings of Caerleon Bridge, River Usk circa. 1811

Both of these pictures illustrate Caerleon as it looked some 200 years ago, the upper view showing the bridge and Roman tower as seen from the marches in about 1815. Below is a view of the wooden bridge leading from Caerleon to Ultra Pontem which was first published in March 1800.

Above is an etching by John George Wood which was published in the folio 'Principal Rivers of Britain' in 1811 shortly after construction of the bridge was completed in 1810.

Hanbury Arms

From about the year 1900 comes this photograph which shows the riverbank, wharf wall and slipway. The Hanbury Arms is in the foreground where it had stood since 1565 having been built as a home for the affluent Morgan family, before being converted into an inn some 200 years later.

The effluent pumping station on the banks of the river in 1972. The effects of the pollution so caused were finally stopped with the banning of discharge directly into the waters and a completely new and large underground piping system to Newport for treatment was constructed.

The paddle steamer 'Albion' of the P.A. Campbell White Funnel Fleet. This was a regular caller to Newport, docking at the floating pontoon near the town bridge to take holidaymakers on excursions along the Welsh coast and Bristol Channel. The postcard photo was provided by the Huxtable Brothers, Newport, well known commercial photographers and issued in 1909 as an April Fool Joke. The hoax being of course that neither the town bridge or Caerleon bridge were high enough to allow passage up the river. The background is of special interest with river wall wharf and slipway in very good condition.

River Bridge and Hanbury Arms
wharf remains circa. 1960

The river bridge and wharf remains as they looked in the early 1960s. Situated just beyond the slipway is the stone-built structure which was used as a transit warehouse by shipping, using the jetties up until the 1890s after which time it was used for general storage by the Hanbury Arms Inn.

By the late 1970s this ancient piece of history belonging Caerleon's shipping era had reached a ruinous state and was eventually demolished.

A scene from the 1970s taken at the junction of Castle Street and High Street and looking towards the bridge. Noticeable is the absence of the *'Long House'* on the right.

The year is now 2005 and the design of the Hanbury Coat of Arms has been modernised somewhat in comparison to the one displayed thirty years earlier in the photograph above.

A one-gallon stone beer jar from the Hanbury Arms that has survived almost a century. The brewery was situated at the side of the inn at the former Bridge Street from 1900 to 1920 and brewer and mine host was Mr. John Sherwood. He was an *'Oxford Blue'* always giving purposeful encouragement to members of Newport Rowing Club to hold their meetings at this particular inn.

Richards & Hopkins,

ENGINEERS, IRON & BRASS FOUNDERS,

Britannia Iron Works, Caerleon,

Near NEWPORT, Mon.

Makers of Colliery Winding and Hauling Engines.   Pumps and Hydraulic Machinery.   Improved Briquette Machines, Steam Pipes and Valves, Shafting.

Railway Wagon and Loco. Wheels Re-tyred and Turned . . . . . . at the Branch Works at Newport.

PROPRIETORS OF . . . .

CAERLEON TIN PLATE Co.,

CAERLEON, Mon.

Makers of Finished Black Plates.

Telegraphic Address :
"Britannia, Caerleon."

National Telephone :
Newport, 52.
Caerleon, 4.

This is evidence that Caerleon was more than capable of maintaining heavy engineering and not being entirely rural years ago. Richards and Hopkins had their foundry close to Brades housing development that we know today.

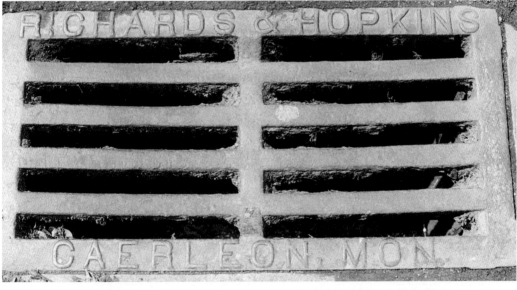

Some further evidence relating to Messrs Richards and Hopkins is this drain cover to be found in White Hart Lane, a surviving 100-year-old piece of Caerleon's industrial history. There are still a number of family relatives of this former company residing in the district.

The Hanbury Garage
1926-1963

During the early years of the 1900s the area of land on, and adjacent to the garage was worked as a smallholding by a Mr. Arnold who lived at the nearby Bridge House. He sold produce from a small shed-type structure known by the name *'Arnold Florist and Fruiterer'*. In 1926 Mr. Reuben Bennett bought a portion of this land utilising the shed of the previous owner and Mr. Bennett a trained plumber, started an engineering and house servicing business. Within two years his business had evolved and had become an established garage for servicing and repair of both motorcycles and cars, together with petrol and oil sales. Reuben's son Gordon took over the business in 1948 and by 1953 had built the bungalow *'St. Christopher's'* that we see near the garage today. In 1955 the remains of the original buildings were demolished

thereby creating the more familiar layout known to all. Gordon continued with the family business until his retirement in 1963 which marked the end of 37 years involvement with the Bennett family. In the photograph which was taken in 1930 an 11-year-old Gordon borrows the Shell-Mex tanker-driver's peaked cap.

> ### *The price of petrol (motorspirit) in 1926 was 1s 6d (equivalent to 7$\frac{1}{2}$p) per gallon.*

Before the arrival of stand-alone fuel pumps, petrol was sold in one or two-gallon cans, a selection of which can be seen here originating from the garage. The period of these cans would be the mid 1920s when the price of petrol stood at 1/6d per gallon so the two-gallon can would have cost 15p in today's decimal currency!

The Garage 1963-2006

Reg Richards with his beloved Golden Labrador, Sandy who were inseparable for 13 years, Sandy dying 12 months after Reg.

Joyce Richards in September 2005 and looking forward to a well-earned retirement after 42 years of service assisted by sons Martyn and Jeffrey.

In October 1963 Reg and Joyce Richards took over the garage up until which time Reg had been running an agricultural and engineering works in Gas Works Lane (now Yew Tree Lane) where he had been servicing the first combined harvesters in the County. In 1998 Reg sadly passed away and Joyce continued running the business whilst also bringing up her three children. In 2005 the decision was made to retire and by January 2006 the garage closed completely, thus bringing 42 years of service to the community to an end.

The First Caerleon Arts Festival International Sculpture Symposium 2003 held at the Hanbury Field

The first Caerleon Arts Festival Sculpture Symposium was held in the Hanbury Field in 2003 with contributions from sculptors around the world. The works of art were photographed by Mr. Ian Irving with their origins numbered accordingly. 1. D. Johnson, UK. 2. A. Rogers, UK. 3. A. Ivanov, Bulgaria 4. S. Vachova, Czech Republic 5. L. Rosinka, Poland 6. E. Harrison, Wales 7. M. Vacha, Czech Republic 8. P. Bews, UK 9. P. Petrov, Bulgaria 10. Zhaolei, China.

All these works of art have now been formed into a Sculpture Trail in the local area.

The idea for the Sculpture Symposium originated with Dr. Russell Rhys in 2002, he having commissioned sculptor Ed Harrison over the previous 10 years with work being displayed at Ffwrwm. Having visited events in the Czech Republic and Germany, he offered the suggestion at a public meeting that it would be of benefit to Caerleon and stimulate tourism in the area and major sponsors and public donation have subsequently supported this very popular annual event. Amongst the many supporters and sculptors of the 2004 event in this photograph are Barbara Gilfillan, Dorothy Kirkwood, Catherine Philpott, PC Sally Convey, Carole Stevens, Catherine Hawke, Norman Stevens, Marilyn Custard, Greville Hunt, Rosemary Butler A.M., *Dave Johnson, Ed Harrison, Michele Valenza,* Tim Davidson, Max Perkins, *Miguel Angel Gualtiera, John Merrell, Juan Carlos Mercurio,* Jenny Perkins, Derek Butler, Catherine Barber, Paul Flynn M.P.
(Sculptors named in italics)

The Stable Yard of Caerleon House - Historic 16th Century Manor

This and the following few pages deal with the historic Caerleon House in High Street. Both pictures on this page were taken in 1985 and show the entrance to the adjoining stable yard which is thought to have been built around 1760. The lower picture which was taken from inside the yard, looks towards High Street when renovations were at an early planning stage.

Caerleon House Stable Yard 1986 which has now evolved into the internationally renowned Ffwrwm Cultural Centre

A year later in 1986 and a celebration is in progress at the opening of the Bric-a-Brac and Antiques Centre. Left to right are Dorothy Kirkwood, Catherine Philpott, Philip Murden, Rita Tait and Russell Rhys. The lower picture shows the interior of one of the stables with a selection of items for sale.

Another section of the stable yard that also shows steps leading to the hay loft. Accompanying Dorothy Kirkwood and Catherine Philpott are two Australian visitors from Melbourne namely Norman and Felicity Raeburn. The lower picture shows Russell Rhys preparing some 'fast food' marking the opening of High Street after repair work and the re-profiling of the carriageway with granite cobblestones.

'Merlin' a sculpture by Ed Harrison displayed at Ffwrwm Art Centre.

As seen here, by 1986 the ancient buildings had received a great deal of care and restoration work presenting a whole new appearance to the premises, where previously, years of neglect had been allowed for it to fall into disarray.

An enthralled audience listens to Alan Barrow telling the story of 'Rhianon' Queen of Dyfed from the Mabinogion, with the sculpture of the claw representing evil magic forces. Amongst the audience, left to right, are Dr. Russell Rhys, Brigadier Robert Aitken OIC Army in Wales, Alan Barrow, Miguel Santiago, Rita Tait, Dorothy Kirkwood, Gillian Rhys, Cllr. Graham Powell, Bethan Lewis, Greville Hunt, Mary England, Rafi Hayon, Carole Stevens, David Jones. The sculpture was created by Ed Harrison of West Wales.

Caerleon's War Memorial was unveiled in May 1921, it taking two and a half years after the end of The Great War to raise the necessary funds for its completion. This picture was taken when it was situated in front of Barclays Bank in 'The Firs' building, before being re-located to its present position in the Memorial Garden in 1966. The names of twenty-eight local men of varying ranks including one merchant seaman are inscribed on the bronze plaque.

A picture illustrating a Caerleon scene from the winter of 1981-1982 when one of the worst storms of the century hit south Wales in January 1982. With no traffic moving, a giant snowman was erected near The Bull.

Yet another scene of change for the town whereby the former Café and Tea Shoppe has acquired new ownership and become the Tabard Brasserie.

August 6th 2004 saw the retirement of David Jones as Caerleon's postmaster, a position he had held for 29 years. Accompanying him in the picture are wife Carol and son Matthew who also contributed greatly to this efficiently-run business in the town.

September 2003 and the popular open-decked 'Discover Newport' bus delivers and collects passengers and sightseers on its circular tour of the district.

Cross Street in 1905 and the premises on the immediate left belong to Mr. W.J. Bennett and his Norman Cycle and Motor Works with a gentleman stood outside a wine and spirits retailer next door. On the opposite side of the street is Miss Clara Jenkins, a general dealer and further up the street and stood in his doorway is the then postmaster Mr. Edwin Green. Cross Street was a busy place in Edwardian times, there being a wide range of grocers, drapers and butchers to choose from.

Backhall Street looking to Church Street

Backhall Street in about 1910 with a view facing The Square. Church Street is on the right with the London Inn directly in front and the Red Lion on the left whilst to the rear right stands the Methodist Church.

Sadly the closure of another former exclusive shop for the town was The Artavia Gallery and proprietor Louise Horton is seen here on the final day of trading in Cross Street in October 2003. The viewing customers are Madaleine Daniel, Doreen Vickery and Margaret Morse.

Refugee children of the Spanish Civil War

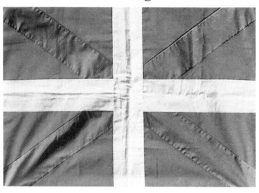

The Basque flag with red background, white cross and green diagonals.

The flag of Wales.

Sunday morning, October 17th 2004 saw the gathering together of friends, relatives, civic dignitaries and former refugee children to mark and commemorate their stay and help given by the people of Wales during the conflict of the Spanish Civil War. The contingent for Caerleon arrived on the 10th July 1937, establishing their colony at Cambria House. Subsequently at the outbreak of World War Two in September 1939, it was commandeered by the Army and the children were re-housed at nearby Vale House, the former infirmary. As many eventually drifted back to their families in Spain, the remaining 30 formed a small community at 18 Cross Street (Pendragon House), led throughout by Mrs. Maria Fernandez and a number settled in Caerleon and around the United Kingdom for good.

Interested supporters are awaiting the unveiling of the 'Basque Children of '37 Association' plaque and amongst the crowd are Keith Richards (with stetson hat), Cllr. Ray Davies (holding Welsh Flag) and Wendy Lewis.

The ceremony is in progress at Number 18 Cross Street when Deputy Mayor Cllr. Alan Morris delivered a moving speech. Left to right are Cllr. Gail Giles, James Kirkwood, Natalia Benjamin and Norman Stevens.

Former Chairman of Gwent County Council and Newport Councillor James Kirkwood with more than forty years of community service behind him speaks on behalf of Caerleon and District Civic Society.

Representing those Welshmen who fought with the International Brigade, Cllr. Ray Davies of Caerphilly and Wendy Lewis sang a tribute song 'Only Our Rivers Run Free' both being members of the Red Choir (Wales).

Master of Ceremonies Norman Stevens delivers a speech on behalf of Caerleon & District Civic Society with an invitation to congregate at the Town Hall for refreshments and view a photographic display relating to the children's stay at Caerleon.

Accompanied by Deputy Mayor of Newport Alan Morris and his wife Jane, Cllr. Gail Giles prepares to unveil the plaque at the express wish of Josefina Savery (nee Alvarez). Gail's dissertation for her degree had as its subject the history of the Basque children in Caerleon. On the day, her speech gave a brief outline of the events and traumas the children and their parents faced during the Civil War and the welcome and hospitality they received after arriving in Wales.

CAERLEON AND DISTRICT CIVIC SOCIETY

CROESO

PENDRAGON HOUSE
18 Cross Street

From November 1939 this building was home to 30 Basque refugee children from the Spanish Civil War who were cared for by local organisations and volunteers. From 1937 to 1939 they stayed at Cambria House, Mill Street.

EUZKADI

BASQUE CHILDREN OF '37 ASSOCIATION. UK

Former residents (when they were children) meet for the ceremonial unveiling of the commemorative plaque outside Pendragon House and in the picture, from the left are Herinio Martinez (Nino), John and Carmen Kilner (Basque Children's Association Committee), Laura Williams (Garcia), Paula Hanford (Felipe), Caerleon Nina, Angelita Clarke (Felipe), Caerleon Nina, Manuel Moreno (Association President), Helvecia Hidalgo, Nina, Josefina Savery (Alvarez), Caerleon Nina, Gerardo Alvarez, Caerleon Nino, Alvaro Velasco, Nino, Natalia Benjamin (Association Secretary), Pauline Fraser, IBMT, Enrique Garay, Nina, Juan Moreno (Association Committee), Tom Webb (Association Auditor): (Nino Spanish for little boy and Nina for girl).

A 1970's picture taken in Cross Street when a few of the Morris dancers appear to be defying the laws of gravity and providing a fine advertisement for Levitation Ale! Also to be seen here are two former shops such as L.G.Avery the butcher's and a small branch of the 'International' supermarket chain, a company better known to shoppers these days as 'Somerfield'.

The 'New Hall' as pictured in 1938. This corrugated metal building was erected in 1931 on Church Street at the junction with Norman Street and was used extensively for community events. Being fully equipped with kitchen facilities it was much utilized for private functions such as wedding receptions, a meeting place for a number of local club activity and headquarters for Caerleon's scout troop.

Crowds are gathered outside the hall ready to disperse following a fancy dress party in the early 1950s. Notice too that an extra high gas lamp is still in use.

Here is a shop on the corner of Backhall Street as seen in 1923 with some renovation work going on next door; many years later it was to become 'Gaslight Antiques' (Val Burnell-Jones). Two young ladies have been identified on the photograph as Betty Vickery (née Edwards) and Barbara Wilkinson (also née Edwards).

The 'Midland Bank' as it was then known in 1980. The Hong Kong and Shanghai Banking Corporation bought an interest in the Midland Bank Ltd. in 1980, later acquiring full ownership and renaming it all HSBC in 1999. Thus another British institution fell into foreign ownership after 150 years of trading.

A drawing of Val Burnell Jones' antique shop front by renowned illustrator and artist Penny Dale in 1984 captures wonderfully the atmosphere of Val's establishment.

Val is seen modelling some of her collection of Victorian and Edwardian ladies apparel at the Roman Festival during the opening of the museum which was held in the grounds of the Priory Hotel in 1987.

A further selection of latter-day costume is displayed by Val Burnell Jones and Anne Collins-Vicary at the Festival and Victorian Fair in 1987. Val specialised in these wares from 1980 to 1996 when ill health forced her to give up what was a fascinating hobby and business. Local residents will remember her as a very popular lady who followed a number of pursuits with much determination and pleasure such as voyaging to the Antarctic, hang-gliding and not forgetting driving her MG and Mercedes sports cars rapidly around the district. The lower photograph shows examples of how the younger generation of Caerleon dressed a hundred years ago.

High Street - The Malt House changing through the years

Standing alongside what is reputed to be the first petrol-dispensing pump in Caerleon is Mr. Billy Bennett, proprietor of the Motor Vehicle Servicing and Charabanc establishment. This business was located in the High Street at the Old Malt House opposite the Priory Hotel and nowadays the Caerleon Kitchen Centre. These were early days for petrol retailers, no electric pumps and the one seen here would have been manually operated by swinging the lever in a side to side motion. Fire and safety regulations were also not a great priority as Billy quite nonchalantly has a cigarette between his lips. The era of this photograph is probably the late 1920s but the old pump was still to be seen as late as the 1970s when the premises were being used by C.M. Pattison Engineering Ltd as recalled by Howard Wookey who served his apprenticeship there.

The old building is still standing and in use here in 1975 when it was purchased by Andsel Thom Ltd who were engineering architects and designers, they converting it into offices and company headquarters.

Two interior photographs of the Malt House and when viewed from both ends it can be seen that there is much work to be done, but the potential is there as any property developer will know!

The renovated exterior

By April 1979 when these pictures were taken time and expense had been invested to restore the building completely where it stands opposite the Priory in High Street.

Knighton Cottage, High Street

The venue is Cardiff Castle in 1983 when Caerleon artist and sculptor Frank Abraham of Knighton Cottage, High Street shows his commissioned work to HRH Princess Margaret. This mural is situated opposite one of the remaining sections of the Roman walled fort built in the 3rd century A.D. and is made of cement and plaster, finished in metallic gold. Depicting Silurian village life in the early first century, it also features the sighting of the Roman fleet off the south Wales coast, followed by men at work in the armoury and the gathering of the Silures to ward off the invaders.

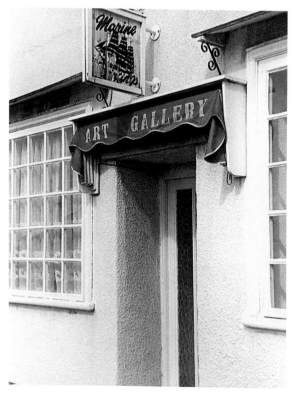

CASTELL CAERDYDD

CARDIFF CASTLE

Knighton Cottage in July 2000. Part of the building was converted into an Art Gallery in 1975 providing a much appreciated amenity for the town and principally designed to exhibit the works of owner Frank Abraham. Originally trained as a commercial artist, his talent developed into a wider dimension but problems with ill health subsequently forced the decision to close the gallery in 1976 and the cottage reverted back to a private dwelling.

Llangibby Hunt Meet on Goldcroft Common, December 4th 1936

December 4th 1936 and the Llangibby Hunt meet outside the Drovers Arms for what was an annual and well-attended event. The Drovers seen in the background shows the sign Lloyds Ales and Stout Newport and not Lloyd and Yorath which might have been expected as it was William Yorath who founded the brewery in 1860 and remained the owner until 1893. At that point a Mr.Lloyd joined the firm as a partner, providing new substantial financial backing, supposedly therefore giving him the right to have his name uppermost wherever possible. This old Newport company was eventually incorporated into the Courage group during the 1960s.

The Annual Chariot Race, Goldcroft Common 1988

The effort made to recreate 'The Race of Old' is impressive as the participants make ready here on the Common. A great deal of work has gone into chariot making, a wide variety of costumes and even a Viking has made a guest appearance.

Heading up High Street via the Square, the charioteers battle through a hail of missiles, water, flour grenades and eggs. Unfortunately this activity would lead to traffic hold-ups and laborious street cleaning afterwards so the decision had to be taken put an end this part of the event despite its huge popularity. The race has however since been revived thanks to organisation by Caerleon Rugby Club using the Fosse Field, thus making it a more acceptable and splendid day out.

In the late 1960s or early '70s this picture reminds readers and local residents of the road sign restricting access but at least traffic was allowed to travel in either direction, there not being the volume of cars as to be seen nowadays.

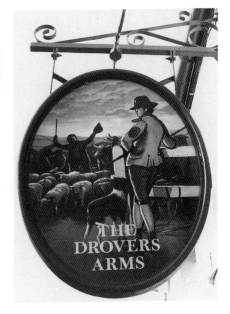

Early days of the Legionary Museum

An etching of the museum prepared shortly after its opening in 1850, the site having been given to the Caerleon Antiquarian Association by local benefactor John Edward Lee. The Association ran the museum itself for 80 years until 1930 when it was handed over to the National Museum of Wales.

The interior of the museum during the 1950s with display cabinets of a very formal fashion. The four columns are additional interesting features, they being former ship masts that were salvaged from the battle cruiser HMS Collingwood which was broken up by Cashmore's the renowned Newport ship-breakers in 1922. The masts were retrieved from the yard on the banks of the Usk and donated to the museum by local builder Mr. Golledge.

A paperweight with the motif of the Second Augustan Legion. The photograph on the left show stone columns formerly part of the medieval market building which was located near the Bull Inn on the Square. Described as being of 'Tuscan Order', low and massive, they are believed to be Roman in origin and these days are preserved at the rear of the museum, whilst in these photographs, they are seen being used to support the ground floor of the original museum. The market building was demolished in about 1845, some of the material then being used to construct the Legionary Museum on land leased from Sir Digby Mackworth.

February 1999 and some re-profiling of the highway is in progress providing greater safety for visitors to the museum. Notice that the original portico has been retained and incorporated into the new building after the old was demolished in 1986.

St. Cadoc's Church

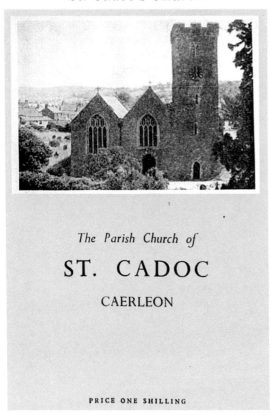

The Parish Church of

ST. CADOC

CAERLEON

PRICE ONE SHILLING

The vicars of Caerleon Church

1254	*Andrew*
1287	*Nicholas de Leycester*
1288	*David de Caerleon*
1398	*William Richard*
1398	*James Fitz Hugh*
(1481)	*John ap Jenkin*
(1491)	*Walter*
(1535-1544)	*William ap Levan*
(1560)	*Thomas Lanne or Langley*
(1590)	*William Mathew*
1595	*Edward James M.A.* (1)
1610	*David Price*
	George Robinson
1660	*Edward Wrinch B.A.*
1662	*Lewis Lloyd*
1663	*Morgan Thomas*
	Charles Hutchings
1700	*Philip Hawkins M.A.*
	Thomas Lingen M.A.
1716	*Griffith Davies*
1728	*Lacon Lambe M.A.*
1742	*Dent Davies M.A.*
1768	*Thomas Mills Hoare M.A.*
1783	*John Thomas B.A.*
1829	*Daniel Jones*
1857	*Howell Powell Edwards M.A.*
1885	*Francis Bedwell B.D.*
1906	*Frederick William Garforth Whitfield M.A.*
1933	*Hugh Owen Williams M.A.*
1949	*Ivor Davies B.A.*
1964	*Douglas Morgan Jones B.A.*
1976	*Philip R.S. Morgan M.A.*
1995	*Arthur Edwards B.A. M.Phil.*

Canon Ivor Davies B.A. 1949-1964

Canon Philip R.S. Morgan M.A. 1976-1995

The choir and vicar pose for a photograph outside the church in 1982. Left to right are: Paul Griffiths, Shaun Moody, Mr. Neville Moody, Ian Marshall, Bill Harris, Mr. Ivor Mathews, Ian Griffiths, Kevin Blackmore, Mr. Len Blackmore, Stephen Prideaux, Simon Maggs, Hywel Jenkins, Paul Harris, David Hills, Alyn Jenkins, Mr. J.H.L. Williams (Church Warden), Chris Comfort, Dean Crighton, Mathew Perkis, Ian Brunning, Mr. Max Morrish (Town Clerk), Adam Cox, Mr. Douglas Davies (Dep. Organist), Mathew Moody, Robert Macintosh, Gareth Jenkins, Martin George, Andrew George, Julian Collingbourne, Dr. Geoff Tyler, Mr. Geoff Jenkins (Organist and Choirmaster), Mr. Gerald Purkiss, Tim Ford.
Standing centre back row: Canon Philip R.S. Morgan (Vicar of St. Cadoc's). Those who may be seen wearing ribbons and medals denote Royal School of Church Music Awards.

Reverend Frederick William Garforth Whitfield M.A. who was vicar at Caerleon from 1906 to 1933 and actually served as a priest for a total of 48 years.

Rev. Beatrice Musindi. B.D., M.A. commenced at St. Cadoc's June 2004 as Assistant Curate, she was born in Uganda.

The period is around 1905 along High Street with Museum Street to the right. Visible on the corner in front of the wall is a block, which was strategically placed to protect the corner of the wall from passing horses and carts whose wheels were frequently causing damage when turning left into High Street. Notice too the ornate cast-iron gates and railings at the church entrance.

An alternative view of the church that was taken during the early 1920s with the minarets providing some 'food for thought'.

Carnivals and Parades

The Mayoral Sunday Parade is led by a combined band of the Boys Brigade in July 1989 and taking the salute from the platform are, left to right - Mrs. Samantha Flynn, Paul Flynn M.P., Her Worship Mayor of Newport Rosemary Butler, her consort Mr. Derek Butler and Canon Phillip R.S. Morgan Vicar of St. Cadoc's.

Entering St. Cadoc's Church to celebrate her inauguration as Mayor of Newport, Caerleon resident Rosemary Butler is seen accompanied by consort Mr. Derek Butler and Cllr. James Kirkwood F.R.S.A.

Against the traffic flow in the early 1960s the Boys Brigade Drum and Bugle Band from Newport proudly and smartly lead the parade to St. Cadoc's Church on the occasion of a service marking the newly appointed Chairman of Caerleon U.D.C. On the left can be seen the fish and chip shop prior to its development and as a Chinese Restaurant.

Caerleon's popular library as seen in March 2006 which is located within the grounds of the Comprehensive School, consequently it does have limited facilities including parking and would quite likely benefit from some relocation eventually. The following pages provide some interior views of the building.

February 2002 and Jean James is seen coping with modern computer technology which has replaced the antiquated systems such as cards and tickets etc. that were used to control the whereabouts and return of library books. In the scene below are Sylvia Parsons and Jean James, two long-serving librarians in the service of the community.

St Cadoc's Hospital Construction

The upper picture shows the period to be mid 1905 when construction of a section of St. Cadoc's Hospital is well underway. The lower photograph shows progress being made although the clock tower still has to be completed with the addition of its timepiece.

The main hospital wings have now been completed, the clock has been installed and all that remains to be done prior to the official opening in 1906 is the clearing of the builders' debris by horse-drawn wagons as seen on the left of the picture.

A close-up of the hospital's clock face reveals some confusing Roman numerals for time watchers. The figures 9 and 11 can be seen as both showing XI when of course 9 should read as IX and 11 as XI; fortunately perhaps, we nearly all look at the position of the hands on a clock face of this size, rather than any numbers.

The main administration building as pictured in May 2003 with little change to its original appearance on the previous page other than the removal of some chimney stacks.

The main driveway entrance to the hospital off Lodge Road, South Lodge adjacent to the railway bridge.

Mr. John Davies (Head Male Nurse) and his wife Edith Mary pose for the cameraman outside their home 'South Lodge' St. Cadoc's Hospital. This gentleman commenced work at the hospital from its opening in 1906 and continued for an incredible 39 years until retirement in 1945.

St Cadoc's Hospital Staff Ball

A typical example of one of yesteryear's forms of entertainment, a programme of dances for the Annual Staff Ball which was held at The Newport Mental Hospital to which St. Cadoc's was referred to at the time in January 1914. This would have been a great social event when dancing, really was dancing, all to a variety of long-forgotten frolics and music. This was a period when it was still customary for ladies to carry a dancing card as seen here, with particular dances reserved for particular partners of their choice; all very much of the highest etiquette.

St Cadoc's Hospital Staff Family Christmas Party

The Hospital Christmas Party for staff and their children was an event very much appreciated and usually held on the first Monday in January with plenty of party food served in the Billiards Room and games and films in the main hall. Dr. King would be 'Father Christmas' with Dr. Douglas Vaughan-Johnston as M.C. In this 1949/50 photograph the following are seen left to right. Front: Royston Hussey, Lyndon Pugh, Colin Crowden, Grosvenor Hussey, Derek Gear, Alan Crowden, Richard Jones, Marion Raines, Francis Pitt. 2nd Row: Valerie Shierson, Frances Rollings, Colin Jones, Andrew Jones, Geraldine Collins, Ted Harrhy, Kathleen Collins. 3rd Row: Ann Wooton, Jeanette Pope, Valerie Jones, Margaret Nelmes, Jeremy Knight, Iris Jones, Tegwyn Pugh (holding Dr. Johnston's son Donald), Glenys Shierson, Maureen Collins, Irene Gittings, Kitty James, Dorothy Atwell, Valerie King, Pamela King, Pat Harris.Back: Keith Hussey, Raymond Raines, Philip Rollings, Kenneth Williams, Raymond Giddings, Ted Gear, Doreen Pritchard, John White, Thelma Rowlands, Nurse, Bob Williams.

Here are two views of Lodge Road from some forty years ago, the upper picture having been taken from inside a car, hence the additional view in the wing mirror! The boundary wall of the hospital has yet to be removed which would provide a safer line of vision for traffic and St. Cadoc's Close and housing is in the course of construction. On the left, boundary walls for the college have also been built. From the opposite direction in the lower photograph there is still some aged gas street lighting in use, complete with vandal-proof barbed wire towards the top.

Lodge Road

Two more views of the Lodge Road area during the 1960s with the upper one showing plenty of open ground where Westgate Court and the Comprehensive School would make their mark in later years. Again from a car interior, a very quiet Lodge Road is seen complete with dated street lighting and the area before the appearance of Westgate Court.

Charles Williams Endowed School

The Caerleon Charity School was endowed by Charles Williams (1633-1720) and built in1724. This picture is from 1986 and shows the head teacher's residence to the left of the main building which was later converted into the school kitchen and subsequently demolished.

In the year 1890 Miss Cross dressed in her school uniform poses with her mother. When the school first opened it was planned for the education of 30 boys and 20 girls between the ages of 7 and 12 (twelve then being a working age for both sexes). Probably due to staff shortages the pupil numbers were reduced to 20 boys and 10 girls, with the decree that lessons should be in strict English only and faithfulness to the established Church. The school uniform was also a stringent affair, consisting of grey coats with CW embroidered in gold, brass buttons also initialled, white collars, waistcoats etc. etc. Girls, as part of their education would make many of their own clothes during lessons. Any spare monies from the endowment were to be used for apprentice indentures.

On the right members of staff at the Boys' School in 1920 with Mr. W.G. Lovett and Mr. C. Francis standing. Seated left to right are Miss C. Stretton, Mr. Evan Davies (Head Teacher 1880-1923) and Miss W. Dean.

Endowed School

A school photograph that probably dates from the 1890s when starched white collars were a 'must' for male pupils and teachers. The gentleman teacher on the far right is a young Mr. Walter G. Lovett.

The period has now moved on to 1931 when Class 2 pay attention to the photographer. Both boys and girls have been instructed to wear the regulation caps with the familiar school badge.

Endowed School

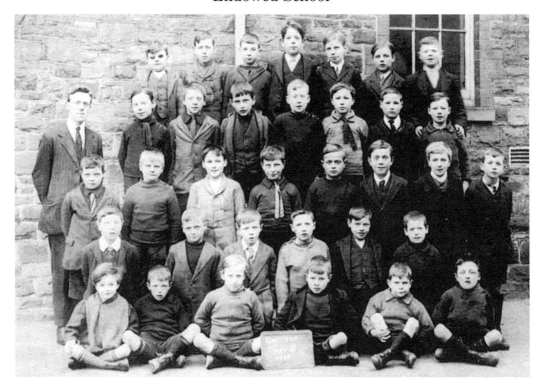

Two pictures taken of the boys' department in 1920 and maybe there are some signs of a relaxation in the wearing of school uniforms, particularly those starched collars and breeches.

Endowed School Christmas Party

A Fancy Dress Party that was held at the Endowed School for Christmas 1932 and standing on the far left with the large hat is Miss Elizabeth Stallard. She had an interesting career which began with her winning a cash prize scholarship whilst a pupil at the school. Aged 16, she assisted at the infants school whilst it was awaiting a new teacher before becoming a pupil-teacher and completing her apprenticeship in 1907 aged 19. She was soon appointed as a non-certificated assistant in the girls school, doing so well that she received fully certified qualifications by 1909. From this she devoted her whole career to teaching, mainly the girls of Caerleon's Endowed School from where she finally retired in 1950 which is recorded on page 45 of 'Caerleon Scenes Changing'.

Christmas spirits are certainly high with an impressive range of costumes for this school concert in about 1936.

The year is believed to be 1962 and here are members of staff who taught the infants at that time. Left to right are - Back: Lillian Edwards, Thelma Cantello and Lillian Cotterell. Front: Kathleen George, Jean Holmes and Ruth Hewitt.

These youngsters are seen in the classroom in 1959 and if any of them are happening to be reading this book, they will probably be wondering where all the years have gone to, now of course being in their 'fifties'. Sandals for boys and girls were the fashion then, with 'trainers' still waiting to be invented!

Seated is headmistress Mrs Kathleen George accompanied by her colleagues Sue Gallagher, Sue Williams and Betty Haswell. Retiring from the infants school in 1983, Mrs George was originally evacuated to Gwent from Dover at the age of 16 in 1940 as the Battle of Britain was about to commence. During her two-year stay in Caerleon and parted from her family, her Dover home was destroyed by shell fire from across the channel. The Caerleon experience led to her desire to become a teacher, which she achieved and married local man Mr Paul George who also joined the profession. In her memoirs Mrs George recalled one very sad incident involving a fellow young Dover teacher Miss Rusbridge. This lady was accidentally killed by a passing lorry close to the Priory Hotel, an event that eventually resulted in the introduction of the one-way traffic system being introduced to the town.

A school trip to London by the junior school led by Primrose Hockey and staff in 1955 and here is the list of known pupils seen left to right. Back: Leslie Barnes, ?, Francis Pitt, George Gravestone, Ann Lewis, ?, Julia Pattimore, Maureen Chick, ?, Robert Vincent, Ann Saunders, Mary Campion, Sandra Johnson, Michael McClure, Tony Bennett, Trevor ?, Keith Edwards. Front: John Harris, Winford Bellin, ?, Yvonne Richards, Gillian Vaulkhard, Geraldine Collins, Valerie Shierson, Janice Vickery, Sylvia Clarke, ?, ?, Wendy Sparkes, Veronica Evans.

This is a summertime school photograph from some forty years ago and virtually all of the pupils' names have been recorded, with sincere apologies for any errors and omissions. Back: Deri Hall, ?, John Wells, ?, Ernest Bowman, Peter Carpenter, Terry Atwell, George Wallen, Keith Hurford, Andrew Jones, Brian Hayward, Lyndon Pugh, Robert Powell, Roger Nicholls, Stuart Dean, Lyndon Raikes, Christopher Pember, Geoffrey Davies, Kenneth Baker. Middle: Caroline Lavender, Diane Edwards, Veronica Jones, Pauline Davies, Julie Thorne, Stephen Wilmott, Leslie Porter, Hugh Green, Glyn Arnold, John Ball, Martin Steed, John Batt, Owen Pugh, Gillian Edwards, Marilyn Chandler. Front: ?, Carol Cooper, Brenda Jeffries, ?, Jennifer Jones, Georgina Powell, Kay Sharples, Kathleen Arthur, Barbara Davies, Rosemary Greenaway, Margaret Morgan, Judith Bellin, ?, Elizabeth Cooper, Wendy Morgan, Margaret White.

In 1956 those in the last year of the junior school were welcomed to the Houses of Parliament by Rt.Hon. Peter Thorneycroft M.P. for the Monmouth constituency who is seen in the back row with Miss Hockey and the pupils and staff include - Back: Veronica Jones, Miss Constance Stretton, Mrs Muriel Meese, Caroline Lavender, Judith Bellin, ?, Josephine Curry, Keith Hurford, ?, Barbara Davies, Kathleen Arthur, Kay Sharples, Wendy Morgan, Jaqueline Winmill, Robert Powell, Julie Thorne, Leslie Porter. Middle: Pauline Davies, Michael Bellinger, Christopher Pember, John Batt, Geoffrey Davies, Lyndon Pugh, Hugh Green, Dennis Bickerton, Elizabeth Cooper, Roger Nicholls, ?, Peter Carpenter, David Adams. Front: George Wallen, John Ball, Rosemary Greenaway, Margaret Morgan, Gillian Edwards, Martin Steed, Terry Attwell, Kenneth Baker, Stephen Wilmott.

The school rugby team for the 1929-30 season and some accompanying teachers who are Mr Wilf Deacon, Mr W.G. Lovett (Head) and Mr Francis. The players are - Back: A. Parker, Jack Evans, Ron Pierce, Glyn Bergum, Arthur Young, ?, John Mapp, Gordon Wilkinson, Tony Powell. Seated: A. Pierce, B. Pierce, Albert Gear, J. Carpenter. Front: ? Carpenter, Jimmy Dixon, Albert Young.

Many years later, comes this football team and teachers in 1971 comprising of the following. - Back: Mr Williams, Colin Gibson, Simon Derrett, Robert Boycott, Mark Davies, Andrew Baldwin, Gareth Tanner, Phillip Owen, Paul Conolly, Mr Havard (Head). Middle: Andrew Stait, Paul Conway, David Stamp, John Strong, Steven Wadley, Malcolm Harris, Craig Richards. Front: Andrew Rollings, Martin Jones.

This time it's the turn of the ladies netball team to be in front of the photographer with teacher Miss Coates far left and headmaster Mr Greener. The players are - Back: Irene Garay, Jackie Stopgate, Pauline ?, Gloria Jones, Margaret ?, Caroline Griffiths. Front: Jill Steed, Jean Pounting, Margaret Morton, Diana Ball, Linda Turner, Angela James, Eluned Williams, Maureen Wills.

A cricket team at the school in 1960-61 is made up of the following boys Back: Tony Baulch, ?, Peter Cook, ?, Michael Taylor. Middle: Bob Blythe, Stephen Phillips, Nigel Miggins, Brian Griffiths. Front: Terry Teague and Donald Prosser.

Clerk to the Charles Williams Charity, Ivor Phillips hands over the keys to a minibus which was bought for use by the Comprehensive School in 1987, the recipient being Mr Phil James Deputy Head. Also in the picture are Mr Neil Ingham and Cllr. Kirkwood chairman of governors.

CAERLEON COMPREHENSIVE SCHOOL
YSGOL GYFUN CAERLLION

Headteacher/Prifathro:
Adrian G. Davies
M.A., M.Ed.

DYFALBARHAD

PERSEVERANCE

Cold Bath Road,
Caerleon, Newport,
South Wales NP18 1NF
Tel/Ffôn : (01633) 420106
Fax/Ffacs : (01633) 430048

A delighted and appreciative group of pupils and staff pose in front of their newly-acquired piece of school transport.

A Christmas Fancy Dress Party that was held at the community hut (now Isca Court) in Lodge Road in 1945 and the author has tracked down a few names, left to right, as follows – Back: U/k, U/k, Edna Ford, Miss White, Nessie Jones, Mrs Poore, Margaret Edwards. Middle: Marjorie Bennett, Nell Thomas, Phylis Pope, U/k, U/k. Front: Sue Reynolds, Mrs Price, Joyce Bennett, Maud Watkins, Hilda Powell.

The years move on and it was 1981 when this Caerleon Carnival was photographed to include the Queen, her court attendants and a number of entrants for the usual display. The picture was also taken inside the community hut.

The Caerleon branch of the Women's Institute under the guidance of Mrs Margaret Ayliffe organized a tableau at the Community Hut to celebrate Empire Day in 1958, as a mark of patriotism. Not all the participants' names have been recalled but here are a few - Back: Alice Eddolls, Gertie Batt, Mrs James, Mrs Thorne, Nicholas Ayliffe, Roger Eddolls, Nora Shierson, Mrs Prosser. Front: Jonathon Ayliffe, John Westlake, Heather George (Welsh Lady), Ann Westlake, Evette Voss, Robin George, Geoffrey Eddolls.

The children of Lodge Hill Junior School were winners of the Cheltenham Music Festival Recorder Competition Cup in 1986 and here is the celebratory photograph. At the back are Mr Frank Harding, (headmaster) and fellow teacher Dawn John. The pupils, starting with the first row in front of their teachers are - Amber Sorrell, Julie Dunk, Kate Griffiths, Siân Davies, Tara Neale, Sonia Lawrence, Sacha Taylor, Shelley Davies. Row 2: Sally Davies, Ruth Scannell, Siân Edwards, Hayley Stokes, Rachel Brunning, Vanessa Williams, Claire Hill, Nikki Powell. Row 3: Amy Ilett, Jaspreet Lottay, Yona Spiteri, Elizabeth Marcussen, Abigail McLaughlin, Caroline Sheen, Claire Wilkie, Christine Harding. Row 4: Liberty Ilett, Catherine Williams, Elinor Clarke, Rebecca Barnes, Sara Lambert, Nicky Garrett, Ruth Hill, Amy McLaughlin, Rachel Stannard, Ceri Malyn. Row 5: Alison Whittaker, Michael Purcell, David Williams, Nicky Rowland, Colin Stanfield, Noel Jeans, Helen Jordan.
Front: Louise Smith who was the individual competition Gold Medal winner.

This is how Gloucester Court, Roman Way looked back in the 1960s with Thorne's General Stores, Harry Thomas the butcher, Chatwins Newsagents and Nicklassons for fruit and veg to be remembered. For the motorist too, there are a few cars in view that may also be recalled from that era such as the Ford Anglia, Mini, Austin Cambridge, Standard Pennant, Vauxhall Victor, Morris 1000 Traveller and Bedford Beagle Van.

The big event of 1951 was the 'Festival of Britain' with parties and parades held around the country. Seen here are Lynda and Derek Turner (aged $3^1/2$ and $2^1/2$) waiting for the procession outside the headmaster's house which was located next to the Industrial School (Cambria House) in Mill Street and established in the year 1859.

The onlookers are gathering in Mill Street for the same event and in the foreground, as part of the walking pageant are Mr Ben Davies (sporting two carrots as a buttonhole) and Mrs Jean Strong as his bride. Stood on the pavement, the lady in the heavy coat is Mrs Barker, wife of John Barker the last GWR signalman at Caerleon box. To the side of Mrs Barker is Doreen Turner holding son Derek with John Andrews and Lynda Turner facing the camera.

The Festival Carnival makes its way through the junction of Mill Street and Backhall Street and leading the way are Caerleon's 'Mayor and Mayoress' for the day, namely Tom Jones (well-known farmer of Penrhos Farm) and John Stamp. The premises in the background with a large window were once owned by a Mrs Jobbins during the 1920s and '30s, trading as the 'Roman City Tea Rooms'. Later, Mr Fred Strong and his wife kept the shop selling faggots and peas, it also served as a sweet shop with sales being made through the bottom half of the window. On the opposite corner was a grocery shop run by Mrs Edmunds and her son Charlie, the building is still there but now converted into a private dwelling. All of the buildings seen in the background were demolished more than forty years ago with the site being developed by the U.D.C. for modern housing. Amongst those stood on the pavement are Robert Reed (with white collar), next to him is Ron Pearce and further along are Mrs Watkins and Elsa Davies.

Another part of the carnival shows these youngsters and their float being overtaken by a once-familiar car, a 1947 Hillman Minx, the float being designed to represent an advertisement for the famous Tate & Lyle sugar cubes.

A portion of the annual carnival of 1955 with a band of kazoo players providing some musical entertainment with Mr Manuel Fernandez stood next to the cyclists looking on. Amongst the players are Barbara Ward, Lyn Pounting, Nellie and Paddy Russell, Ann Raikes, Kathy Nicholson, Lynne Glass, Zena Winmill, Carol Weaver, Irene Garay, Megan Williams.

August 1956 and another carnival float is on parade, this time representing the typical Welsh miner complete with a genuine selection of coals that were once available in years gone by.

Also from the 1956 event Geoff Rowlands portrays Ali Baba and his Forty Thieves in a walking tableau.

Ray Llewellyn is the person heavily disguised as the scarecrow for this particular carnival entry for which he took first prize. Not remembering until the last minute that he was actually taking part, Ray rushed out into his garden and took the clothes off his real scarecrow much to the appreciation of the watching crowd seen here.

The Carnival Queen for 1959 was 16-year-old Sonia Phillips seen here with her attendants Jan Ibbotson, Veronica Keen, C. Spendelow, Billy Teague, Monica Williams as the float pauses for photographs in Broadwalk.

The Carnival Queen's carriage was a classic dray provided by Hancock's Brewery and hauled by two very patient shire horses.

On Goldcroft Common in 1959 the Carnival Queen's mounted escort Denville Stamp is seen in full regalia as he prepares to lead the parade.

Queen Sonia and her entourage are prepared for the banquet and left to right are Monica Williams, Veronica Keen, Sonia Phillips, Jan Ibbotson and Georgina Powell. The two page boys are Christopher Phillips and Billy Teague.

The 1959 carnival was honoured with the presence of the Regimental Band of the Royal Artillery, Territorial Army Newport pictured whilst entering Goldcroft Common from Lodge Road. The lower photograph sees the band passing by the walls belonging to Croft House which nowadays are devoid of the collection of attractive trees.

Winners of the Carnival Cup in 1966 are these lady footballers seen in Backhall Street with most of their names remembered as follows from left to right- Val Burnell-Jones, Val Edmunds, Catherine Nicklasson, Mary Davies, Zena Winmill, U/k, Gwen Morton, May Morton, Mary Nash, Margaret Williams, Mary Ford, Jill Bowden (holding the trophy), Benny Davies, U/k, U/k, Jeff Snook, Cissie Hopkins, Bertie Nicklasson, Edie Nicklasson.

A special carnival was held in the town in May 1937 to commemorate the coronation of King George VI and seen here decorated for the occasion is local milk roundsman and shopkeeper Mr Lad Coopey with one of his tricycle milk carts. In the background is the Primitive Methodist Chapel on Goldcroft Common which was built in 1814 and used for worship until 1933. This building had a number of uses thereafter including a monumental mason's workshop before final demolition in 1950. The site is now occupied by a private dwelling.

Caerleon Retired Persons Welfare Club

Members of the Caerleon Retired Persons Welfare Club are seen on-stage during a performance at the Town Hall in 1992. Left to right are Mrs Williams (pianist), Mrs Parry, Mrs Jones, John Hopkins, Charlotte Raines, Herbert Nicklasson, Lita Jones, Gordon Williams, Emma Buck, Royce Gardener, Ivy Baker, Joe Hall (compere), Ivor Morgan (choreographer). The concert party entertained audiences for fifteen years.

THURSDAY, DECEMBER 18TH, 1884.

CHAIRMAN - - - REV. CANON EDWARDS.

The Proceeds of this Entertainment will be devoted to the Funds of the Caerleon Reading Room.

PROGRAMME.

1. Overture .. .. .. "Masaniello" ... ... *Auber*
   Organ, Mrs. A. Morris; Pianoforte, Bells, and Trumpet—Miss Florence Pennymore and Miss Kate Harrison; Guitar and Nightingale—Miss Brind; Cymbals—Miss Collingdon; Castanets and Cuckoo—Miss Morris; Drum—Miss Cope; Triangle—Miss Pennymore.
2. Trio ... ... "Oh! Happy Fair" ... ... *Shield*
   Miss Kate Harrison, Miss Morris, and Miss Cope.
3. Duett ... . "I know a Bank" ... ... *Horn*
   Mrs. A. Morris and Miss Kate Harrison.
4. Galop .. .. "Sleigh Bells" .. .. *Caldicot*
   The Band.
5. Song ... "The Arab's farewell to his Favourite Steed" —
   Miss Morrris.
6. Song ... ... "Swing Song" ... ... *Jackson*
   Miss Cope.
7. Part Song ... ... "Summer Fancies" ... ... *Metra*
   Miss Brind, Miss A. Brind, Miss Kate Harrison, Miss Cope, Miss Collingdon, and Miss Morris.
8. Song ... ... "Robin Adair" ... ... —
   Mrs. A. Morris.
9. Selection ... ... "Lucrezia Borgia" ... ... *Donizetti*
   The Band.
10. Song ... ... "The Old Song and the New" ... *Marcus Fielding*
    Miss Collingdon.

11. Song ... ..."The Children's Home " ... ... *Cowen*
    Miss Kate Harrison.
12. Recitation ... "The House that Jack built" ... —
    (School Board version) with illustrations.
    Miss Cope.
13. Song ... ... "Down the Long Avenue" ... .. *Molloy*
    Miss Morris.
14. Vocal Waltz ... ... "See Saw" ... ... *Gwylim Crowe*
    The Band.
15. Song ... ... "Home, Sweet Home" ... ... —
    Miss Kate Harrison.
16. Song ... ... "The Old Lock" ... ... *Wellings*
    Miss Brind.
17. Song ... ..."Far away in Dreams" ... .. *Hutchison*
    Mrs. A. Morris.

TO CONCLUDE WITH A GRAND LAUGHABLE

WAX WORK EXHIBITION.

Showman .. Mr. F. Gardner | Assistant .. Mr. A. T. Stephens

"GOD SAVE THE QUEEN."

DOORS OPEN AT 7.30. COMMENCE AT 8 SHARP.

Admission:—Front Seats, 6d.; Second Seats, 3d.; Gallery (for Children only), 1d.

A Conveyance will Leave for Newport at the Close of the Entertainment.

The NEXT ENTERTAINMENT will take place on THURSDAY, JANUARY 8th, 1885.

FRED. GARDNER, } Hon. Secs.
G. W. HARDING, }

There was a keen interest in local entertainment more than a hundred years ago in the town as this programme of events illustrates for the Christmas period 1884, the concert having been held in the Town Hall reading room.

The Caerleon Retired Persons Welfare Club was founded in 1948 and here is a scene from the presentation of long-membership certificates to Florence Pritchard, Nancy Wollan and Joan Bevan. The chairman is Royce Gardener MBE.

The evening was a lavish and well-attended affair and seated in the front of the camera are Allan Whiting, Tom Jayne, Royce Gardener, Florence Pritchard, Molly Spokes and Dennis Spokes.

The parties well supported

Honoured Citizens of Caerleon at Buckingham Palace

Royce Gardener stands before HRH Prince Charles as he is awarded the MBE at Buckingham Palace on February 20th 2004, the citation reading *'Awarded Member of the Order of the British Empire for services to the Police Force (Monmouthshire and Gwent Constabulary). Trustee of Caerleon Pensioners Association. Chairman of Caerleon Pensioners Welfare Club. Life member of the National Association of Retired Police Officers'.*

Born in Abertillery in 1924, Royce Gardener left school at 16 to work in the laboratory at Six Bells colliery. In 1948 he joined the Police Force and worked throughout South Wales, qualifying as an advanced patrol driver, being promoted to sergeant in Abergavenny and later as sergeant in charge at Caerleon. This was followed by being a member of No.8 Regional Crime Squad which meant duties further afield in Wales as a Detective Sergeant, a number of murder cases passing his way. Other duties included secondment as bodyguard to HRH Princess Margaret during the Investiture of the Prince of Wales at Caernarvon in 1969. One of his most painful tasks was during three weeks at the Aberfan disaster of 1966 in assisting the parents' identification of their children. On the left the MBE recipient is pictured with wife Marion at Buckingham Palace.

Mr James Kirkwood is pictured receiving his MBE from Prince Charles at Buckingham Palace on November 14th 2003, the citation reading *'Chair of Governors Caerleon Comprehensive School, for services to education and the community in South East Wales'* Jim Kirkwood was born in Kingston-upon-Hull in 1926 and played an early role in war duties in 1939 acting as an air raid warden cyclist messenger. His first paid occupation was an apprentice draughtsman at the Blackburn Aircraft Factory which produced vital wartime machines such as the Botha, Skua and Roc. When old enough in 1944, he volunteered for the RAF being selected for aircrew as an air gunner, receiving the air gunner winged brevet badge and soon promoted to sergeant. Flying in Wellington and Stirling bombers until the war ended in 1945, put him in good stead as he qualified as an air traffic controller, being posted to Pembroke Dock with Coastal Command. South Wales had by now caught his attention so he decided to stay in the principality, securing a position in the steel industry at Port Talbot before moving on to Llanwern as the plant opened up in 1961 from where he retired in 1981. He was elected to Caerleon UDC in 1962 which was the start of a long political career. He became chairman in 1968, moved on to the Gwent County Council from 1974 and became its last chairman before amalgamation in 1995. Retirement from local politics came in 2004 having served as a councillor for the Caerleon ward on the Newport Borough Council. Jim Kirkwood has been an active and strong supporter of several charities, Aircrew Association, RAF Benevolent Fund, Chairman of Newport R.N.L.I., Member of Caerleon Branch the Royal British Legion etc. and was honoured by being made President of 1367 ATC Caerleon in 2003. Numerous other accolades include chairmanship of Caerleon Comprehensive School Governors, founder member of the Caerleon and District Civic Society and President of Caerleon Rugby Club for some thirty years.

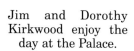

Jim and Dorothy Kirkwood enjoy the day at the Palace.

THIS PLAQUE MARKS
THE PLANTING OPPOSITE OF A CHERRY TREE
BY
COUNCILLOR JAMES KIRKWOOD M.B.E., F.R.S.A.
DONATED FROM HIS COMMUNITY FUND
AND AS BRANCH MEMBER
TO COMMEMORATE THE 80TH ANNIVERSARY
OF THE FOUNDING ON THE 23RD JUNE 1924
CAERLEON BRANCH
THE ROYAL BRITISH LEGION
PRESIDENT GORDON MURRAY, CHAIRMAN HENRY WEST
JUNE 2004

The date is June 20th 2004 when a plaque commissioned by branch member Norman Stevens, was unveiled at the memorial garden to mark the 80th anniversary of the founding of the Caerleon Branch of the Royal British Legion also marked by the planting of a cherry tree on April 6th 2004. In this picture are Alan Whiting (Branch Standard Bearer), Cllr. James Kirkwood MBE, FRSA, Gordon Murray (Branch President) and Henry West (Poppy Appeal Organiser).

Branch members at the unveiling ceremony following a service held at St. Cadoc's Church conducted by Canon Arthur Edwards and the decorated group includes Edward Cooper, Ken Rees, Alan Whiting, James Kirkwood, Henry West, Gordon Murray, Marjorie Murray, Ron Morgan, Jane Burnell, Eric Morgan, John Francis, Victor Morgan.

Ron Morgan RAF seen during his first week of training at Weston-Super-Mare in August 1942 prior to service in Burma, India and Siam.

Henry West who was a flight mechanic from 1940-46 serving principally on the east coast with Blenheims, Beaufighters and Mosquitos.

James Kirkwood in February 1944 as an RAF air gunner, his ambition to become a pilot being thwarted by a *'a lazy left eye'*. He was demobbed in June 1947.

The planting of the commemorative tree on April 6th 2004 with Ron Morgan RAF, James Kirkwood RAF, Henry West RAF and Norman Stevens RN.

Gordon Murray pictured in Iraq in November 1942, whilst in the RAF, his duties also taking him to Iran, Italy and Greece guarding vital airfields.

In the Memorial Room in the Town Hall will be found the Roll of Honour to those Caerleon citizens (men and women) who served in The Great War 1914-18. The total number of names is 139 and of the 17 officers listed, 6 of them bear the name of Mackworth.

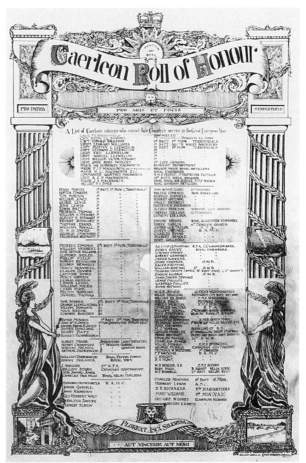

Jim Waggett joined the RAF as a volunteer aged 19 in 1941. After basic training he was posted overseas serving in India, Burma and Ceylon with an aircraft control unit which directed forward fighter operations over Japanese held territories. He was demobbed in July 1946 with the rank of sergeant.

A November morning in 1997 and the children of the Endowed School attend the annual Service of Remembrance in the Memorial Garden. This is a splendid ongoing tradition of participation each year accompanied by the school orchestra conducted by Mrs. James Nicholas with soloists Nicholas Baker and Cathy Nicholas sounding the Last Post.

Lad Coopey is seen wearing his tin helmet, ARP badge and carrying his gas mask alongside Caerleon's makeshift ambulance during World War Two. The ambulances were large saloon cars which were converted by having the rear half of the coachwork removed and a square sectioned bodywork fitted. This was designed to be able to hold two steel tubed stretchers that held lattice wirework for the patient to lie on. The car in itself would be a rarity today, it being an Alvis Silver Eagle with its headlights typically partly blocked to allow the minimum of light so as to avoid detection from enemy aircraft.

An Austin ambulance with the former Monmouthshire registration number AWO 703 belonging to the St. John Ambulance Brigade which was stationed at Cambria House and manned by local personnel.

The period is the late 1940s and on display is the latest Bedford ambulance provided by the Monmouthshire Ambulance Service in the traditional dark blue livery. The bell fixed on the front of the vehicle and a flashing light over the windscreen were the warning signals to other traffic.

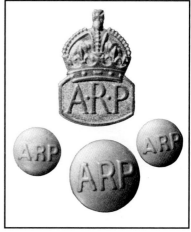

ARP (Air Raid Precautions) lapel badge and buttons as worn on a blue battledress wartime uniform.

The ambulanceman's uniform cap badge which depicts the Monmouthshire Coat of Arms and department name.

The date of this photograph is September 1949 with Mr Lewis (Lad) Coopey and Mr Joe Long dressed in their official ambulance uniforms from that period.

Ambulanceman Mr Doug Glass rests a foot on the running board of his Morris
ambulance outside the garage at Caerleon in September 1949. The livery at this time
was dark blue on all ambulances operated by Mon. County Council. The sole means of
Audible Emergency Warning for other road users was the electrically operated bell on
the bumper with flashing lamp over the cab.

Lad Coopey is stood next to his Bedford vehicle with which he was often sent on
emergencies single-handed. In those days the term 'paramedic' was unknown in the
service and more often than not, the assistance of an attending police officer or
member of the public had to be relied upon to manoeuvre a stretcher.

The period has moved on to the 1970s by which time of course more modern-looking and upgraded ambulances were in service. The crew seen above consists of Graham Smith, Brian Evans, Ron Comfort, Peter Marshall and Jeff Holland.

In 1972 the team won the Welsh Region Cup in the National Ambulance Competition and displaying some trophies are Ron Comfort, Doug Glass, Edgar Davies (Chief Ambulance Officer), Jeff Holland and Peter Marshall.

The families and children are not forgotten by the Ambulance Service as these pictures show. Above, the Christmas Party is underway at Cambria House in 1950 whilst below some fun and games take place on the racecourse.

Mr. Laurie Porter M.B.E. Chief
Officer 1977-1991.

First cap badge issued on
amalgamation with Gwent.

Mr. R.H. Edwards Deputy Chief
Ambulance Officer.

Subsequent badge
issued in 1975. Designed
by competition the
winner being Mr. Reg
Edwards.

The Gwent Ambulance Authority Headquarters, Ambulance Depot and Maintenance
Workshops. Previously under Monmouthshire County Council, the building served as
a Registry Office.

Some more views of the Headquarters area which by this time had been abandoned whilst awaiting demolition and redevelopment for housing. To the right were the workshops and in the foreground the HQ parking area. The stone building roofline to the left is 'Vale House' which was originally built as an infirmary to Cambria House (workhouse) in 1858. In the middle distance can be seen a few houses forming part of the future development of the site.

A view of the garages for ambulances, patient-transport service buses and service vehicles looking up towards Mill Street.

Caerleon Municipal Golf Course was opened in April 1975 and pictured here demonstrating how to get out of a bunker using a lawn edge cutter is Gerald Floyd, a former professional and now green-keeper with Newport Borough Council. Standing by to put the sand back are Nick Smith, John Bevan, Dave Williams and Bentley Morris.

The ladies section of Caerleon Bowling Club as they appeared in 1987 and left to right they are Martha Jane Knorz, Grace Cook, Doris Williams, Mrs Brewer (President), Florence Pritchard, Hilda Bergum, Mabel Gilbert and Emily Beese.

'Ultra Pontem' was a racehorse bought in 1998 as a syndicate interest, named after the local area and raced in colours similar to Caerleon Rugby Club (black and emerald green). The horse had a number of good seasons particularly 2003 resulting in three wins, the first of which was at odds of 50-1 then later retiring to stud, the first foal arriving in May 2006.

Former 1st team Caerleon Rugby Club member Linsey Kirkwood, now the sole owner of Ultra Pontem stands next to jockey Rodi Green in the winners' enclosure Newton Abbot with a few friends sharing the triumph.

A dated but historic photograph of Caerleon A.F.C. soccer team from 1912 and just maybe there are some descendants in and around the district to this day. In the picture are - Back: T. Morgan, F. Mills, A.E. Bolton (Treasurer), N. Davies, H. Bowden, G. Dawes, J. Fitzgerald, J. Davies, W.H. Stewart (Trainer). Middle: A. Attwood, R. Trew, G. Jones, S. Parry, F. Halford, A. Williams, T. Ablart (Hon Sec). Front: A. Perry, J. Neale, W. Hawkesley.

Many years later in 1960, Caerleon were winners of the Monmouthshire Senior League Division One and the gentlemen seen here, left to right, are - Back: Tom Whitfield, Tommy Davies, Glyn Prosser, John Pritchard, D. Eaton, Ray Wilson, Len Wollan, Syd Waggett, Graham Rosser, Ted Marchant, Sid Shaw. Front: Doug Glass, Roy Hill, Lionel Prothero, Glyn Thomas, Alan Jones, Albie Ralph, C. Jones and Bill Roberts.

The Chairman of Caerleon Urban District Council Jim Waggett is seen amidst the team members who helped win the 1960-61 season cup and left to right are - Back: T. Whitfield, L. Prothero, S. Pugh, A. Young, I. Davies, J. Jones, B. Kilvington, K. Edwards, K. Williams, G. Cavaciuti, L. Jones, R. Wilson. Front: G. Dixon, J. Young, A. Ralph, G. Prosser, Jim Waggett, A. Jones, T. Davies, B. Dixon, R. Hill, S. Shaw.

The years have moved on to 1975 and the players pictured outside the clubhouse now are Back: A. Milne, T. Rosser, M. Heames, G. Cavaciuti, P. Griffiths, A. Eagles, P. Clarke, W. Jeremy (Trainer). Front: V. Lewis, R. Shaw, J. Wollan (Captain), T. Teague, J. Cook.

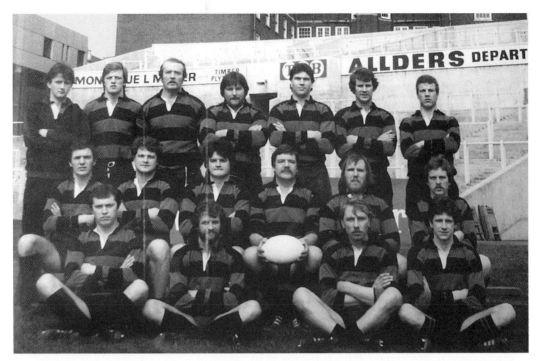

The Caerleon Rugby Team won the Welsh Brewers Cup during the 1980-81 season and here they are on the sacred turf at Cardiff Arms Park. Back: A. Harris, M. Davies, I. Griffiths, D. Morgan, A. Zennadi, G. McCabe, M. Lewis. Middle: F. Headon, J. Jones, P. Morrison, N. Miggins (Captain), P. Macey, R. Derrett. Front: G. McCarthy, L. Kirkwood, D. Allen, G. Gwynne.

April 4th 1981 and Nigel Miggins receives the Welsh Brewers Cup from Mr Cliff Jones the WRU Centenary Season President.

It's back to 1950 and the champion dart players from the Hanbury Inn receive the winners cup during a presentation evening. Most of the names have been recalled as follows, left to right - Ernie Goddard, Gordon Williams, Charlie Williams, William Povall (Chairman Caerleon UDC), ?, ?, Ron Price (Builder), Ray Llewelyn, John Turner (Happy Snaps), Bobby Williams, ?.

The year on this occasion is 1956 and the darts team and their wives join in a celebration. Around the table are Betty Waggett, Joan Williams, Kath Llewelyn, Ray Llewelyn, Sid Waggett, Gordon Williams, Bob Williams, Vera Waggett, Ron Westren and Rita Williams.

Here is an event deemed important enough to attract a large number of spectators in the early 1920s – a road-running race probably heading in the direction of Newport. The cyclists are dressed in everyday attire and are accompanied by a St. John Ambulance Brigade first-aider, suggesting the race to be of some distance although only one lonely runner is in the photograph in front of the St. John cyclist. The Angel Hotel is prominent with a shop on the corner by Mill Street and to the right, beneath the sign 'Teas' , the roof of the No.2 service bus to Newport can be seen. This was the departure point, having turned into Lodge Road from High Street then into Broadwalk, into Station Road then into Goldcroft Common. Those were days when High Street was able to cope with two-way traffic.

An article taken from the South Wales Argus of October 13th 1942 recording a local event that caused a stir at the time.

Caerleon Thrill, Horse dashes into Hotel

This is the story of five minutes excitement at Caerleon. A horse to which a milk float was attached and on which rested churns of milk suddenly took fright in Station Road Caerleon and bolted. Down Station Road the animal charged at forty miles an hour according to one witness. Ahead was the Angel Hotel, on the opposite side of the Newport-Usk main road, a lane and nearby a Newport Corporation Bus with passengers aboard. The bus driver Mr George Prosser of 20 Sutton Road, Newport, observing the possible danger to the bus, drove it out of harm's way and at that minute the runaway animal reached the main road. The horse appeared to suddenly decide that it had gone far enough and said Mr Prosser to an Argus reporter, skidded at speed into the door of the hotel. The door which is narrow, was fastened on the inside but so severe was the impact that the horse smashed clean through. People rushed to the rear of the hotel to get through to the front door and help the horse but it was at the back door almost as soon as the helpers who had been expecting to find the beast injured. The animal which belonged to Mr F. George of Broadway, Caerleon had walked right through the hotel, totally unharmed and was ridden away. The float however was badly damaged and quite a quantity of precious milk lost.
As the saying goes 'No good ever came from crying over spilt milk'.

Delivering the Milk

Station Road and a winter's day in 1938 with milkman Harry Sevenoaks on his round. From the churns, milk would be dispensed straight into the housewife's own jug using ½ or 1 pint ladles. It was always good practice to keep the customer happy by giving the milk in the churn a good swirl before serving to ensure everyone had a fair share of the cream which always rose to the top. The lower picture shows Harry turning his horse and Caerleon Dairy cart in the middle of a very quiet and traffic-free Station Road.

The story of a family business - Marjorie and Laddie Coopey

Marjorie was born in Holbeck, Leeds on June 14th 1912. Her mother, Louisa Storey was from Caerleon and father John Archer Storey from Leeds, who tragically died at the very young age of 35 in 1915. The family returned to live in a cottage on the common in Caerleon with Granny Bolton, Louisa's mother. This was a small cottage and certainly not large enough to accommodate two families so Louisa moved with her children into a flat above the shop in No.2 Station Road. Eventually Mr Lewis William Coopey bought the house and shop here and he, his wife and son also named Lewis (known as Lad which derived from the comments made by the Scottish midwife at his birth as being *'a bonny wee laddie'* and helped distinguish which Lewis was which) moved in with the Storey family moving to No.3 High Street, the cottage vacated by Mr and Mrs Coopey.

When old enough, Marjorie went to work in the shop for the Coopeys who also ran a thriving milk round which operated from the dairies at the rear of the premises at 2 Station Road; she worked hard in both the shop and dairy with Mrs Coopey. The adjoining shop which was their property was before the war used as a bank and Marjorie used to clean the premises and make tea and coffee for the manager. The bank eventually became a hairdressers - Marjorie Davies, then a newsagents and is now a beauty salon, a far cry from the shop of old. In 1935 Marjorie and Lad were married and produced two daughters in 1936 and 1940. The shop was a tobacconist and confectioners and the dairy sold milk with any milk leftovers being made into ice cream by the ladies.

It was a cold job at the best of times but in wintertime even more so and Lad would be out on his rounds twice every morning. The milk came from Mr Skinner's farm on the Chepstow Road, Newport being delivered in the evening and again in the early morning so the first customer delivery would be very early morning and the second straight after breakfast. The milk would be put into whole or one-third pint bottles which had all been hand-washed by Mrs Coopey and Marjorie in the second of the dairies, the first one being used for storage. The smaller bottles were delivered to the schools, about 300 of them for the pupils. Milk was delivered to household customers by churns, Lad filling their jugs with a special handled tin jug or by milk boys on bikes fitted with baskets to carry the bottles, the bottles in those days having a cardboard stopper placed in the top. The third dairy building was used for storing the boys' bicycles.

Eventually Lad bought a BSA three-wheeler car and life became a little easier for delivering at least, whilst things remained just as busy for Marjorie and her mother-in-law. The ice cream was only produced on days when they knew they would be able to sell it quickly as they didn't possess a refrigerator in the early days. When refrigerators did become the norm, the Lyons Maid ice cream factory supplied the equipment so home-made ice cream was to be no more. To advertise the ice cream a rather large artificial cone was placed on the pavement outside the shop with one of the favourite ice creams on the top - the one which was circular with a piece of paper wrapped around the side of it; delicious when unwrapped and no sticky fingers.

Upstairs at No.2 Station Road was a huge room which used to double up as a cricketers tea room for quite a few years, teas being provided by Marjorie and the other girls who served in the shop.

Eventually the war came and Lad had to join the army. He volunteered for the Tank Regiment but was turned down due to his defective eyesight, a childhood injury at five years of age. He was thus transferred to the Royal Pioneer Corps where he attained the rank of Full Corporal. The milk business had to be sold but the shop was still run by Marjorie with the help of her mother-in-law. Marjorie's name was then put above the shop and thus she became the shopkeeper. This proved to be hard work as the shop was open from early morning until late at night with commodities being very scarce or rationed. She managed quite well however until Lad came home from the army when he had to find work, which he did so as an ambulance/clinic driver for Monmouthshire County Council. Before the war the shop window was dressed by window-dressers from the large sweet and tobacco companies with whom the Coopeys dealt and was a sight to behold, but during the war it became very difficult due to material shortages so it was left to the family to make do with whatever was available. The shop sold a variety of things such as birthday cards which Marjorie kept in an album under the counter along with fruit pastilles, wine gums, Smith's crisps, shoelaces, cotton etc.etc. During rationing, the difficult thing was counting the coupons which was undertaken in the room behind the shop and woe betide anyone opening the door quickly causing a draught, which would send the strips of coupons all over the place.

Lad and Marjorie enjoyed some leisure time going out in the car, off to dances and most of all going to whist-drives all over the countryside. They were a well-known couple in many small villages - firstly for delivering milk, then for their attendance at local whist-drives and dances and then Lad as he became the driver of the clinic van that travelled out into the countryside with doctors and nurses on board seeing to the needs of the country-folk.

Marjorie was a member of the Young Wives in the town for many years and then joined the Red Cross and helped raise funds for the cause, being awarded a Certificate of Merit of which she was very proud. When she moved from Goldcroft Common after Lad's passing (they having moved there in 1960 after selling the shop) to Westgate Court, she continued her work with the Red Cross and helped to organize many whist-drives in the Town Hall. Her love of dancing also continued and did so until she was into her eighties. Lad and Marjorie's lives centred on Caerleon, the family and the shop all through their marriage and before - they knew no other town like theirs and loved their surroundings and the people who all knew and loved them.

Marjorie died in August 2005 aged 93 and the funeral service was held in St. Cadoc's Church conducted by Canon Arthur Edwards before a capacity congregation. Lad's father Mr Lewis William Coopey was quite a character in the village (like his son), he owning several houses and helped build the New Hall which was quite a feature during the war years and well into the fifties. The New Hall dances and whist-drives were very well-attended and enjoyed by many. Mr Coopey also built a set of garages on land up the lane off Normans Lane which he rented out for keeping bicycles and cars. He spent a lot of time there repairing bikes for everyone and would often be seen in the town riding his own cycle. Although he bought his son quite a few cars, he never learned to drive himself, much preferring to handle a horse and trap which he did for many years. His love of horses meant he liked to follow Point to Point races and go to Chepstow Racecourse dressed in his Harris Tweed suit, carrying his shooting stick - quite the country gentleman. His other loves included the whist-drives and watching Caerleon cricket team in action of which he was a strong supporter albeit suffering from hay fever meant missing a fair bit of the action.

Col. Sir William Crawshay D.S.O., E.R.D., T.D. Vice Lord Lieutenant of Gwent presenting the Certificate of Merit to Majorie Coopey.

Lad Coopey is on the tricycle and Harry Sevenoaks on the milk cart in about 1930. The cart must have been a recent acquisition as it still displays 'Gilwern Farm Dairy' on the side.

Where Lad was born at No. 3 High Street in 1935 with a young helper, which was then the family home. Also in the picture is Tony Powell a lamplighter.

Also from 1938 this picture was taken near Station Road, junction with Broadwalk. This young man reputedly took the corner a little too fast one morning and deposited the milk onto the roadway.

August 1938 and Lad Coopey poses in his new BSA three-wheeled motor car outside the Endowed School. Notice the stack of milk crates occupying the passenger seat!

Marjorie in the company of Ben the sheepdog in 1992.

Above is an example of a 1950s milk bottle bearing the company name.

This picture dates from about 1935 with a classic car from the period - a Morris Cowley. Marjorie Storey (née Coopey) is at the wheel accompanied by Lad. Sat in the back are Mr Phil Phillips of Bulmore Farm with Ivor Gough.

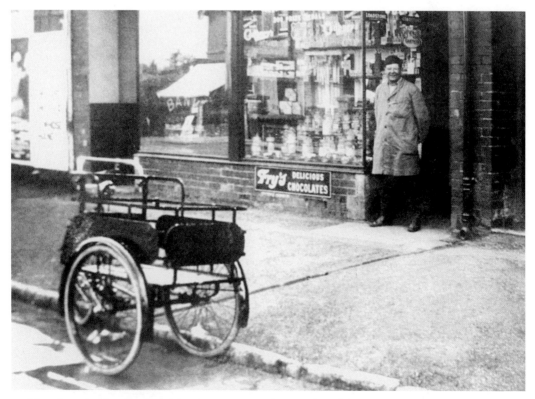

The shop in Station Road in the 1930s with a smiling Mr Lewis (Lad) Coopey in the doorway.

Coat of Arms GWR buttons that were issued up until 1900.

Thomas Chick Strange who was stationmaster at Caerleon from 1884-1896. Lodging in Backhall Street, he married one Rosa Poulson whose parents Daniel and Matilda were local business people as coal merchants, hauliers, market gardeners and also ran the London House Inn. Thomas Strange had a very successful career with the Great Western Railway Company before retiring as stationmaster of Pontypool Road responsible for all passenger and goods departments. The clock seen here was presented to him on the occasion of his marriage such was his popularity with the travelling public. He died in June 1929 aged 75 and the clock remains as a family heirloom in the possession of his grandson Canon Philip Morgan formerly of St. Cadoc's Church.

THIS CLOCK WITH A PURSE OF GOLD
WAS PRESENTED TO
Mr T. Strange, Station Master, Caerleon.
ON THE OCCASION OF HIS MARRIAGE
BY THE INHABITANTS OF
CAERLEON.
AS A MARK OF THEIR APPRECIATION OF THE COURTESY SHOWN BY HIM
IN THE DISCHARGE OF HIS OFFICIAL DUTIES. Aug 28TH 1887.

CAERLEON

A non-stop express train heads north through St. Cadoc's cutting and fast approaching Caerleon station; also seen are the branch lines. On the lower left of the picture are the branch lines leading to the goods yard. At the top of the photograph is the station 'totem' platform sign which would have been chocolate brown and cream enamel.

Diesel powered locomotives gradually replaced the ageing steam trains in the mid 1950s and seen here is a multiple unit waiting on the down platform on its way to Newport High Street.

GWR locomotive No. 2837 passes at some speed past the down platform in the 1950s and the single lamp on the buffer beam signifies that this is a 'light engine' i.e. an engine only and no rolling stock.

Powdered cement was used in mass quantities during the construction of the Spencer Steelworks at Llanwern, part of which arrived at Caerleon station goods yard. Here a load awaits transfer into an Albion cement in bulk lorry seen with its cylindrical container for the cement powder for delivery to the new works in 1960.

Scenes from the goods yard in 1962 when coal was 'King', with truckloads of the main heating fuel belonging to the period having been delivered and awaiting collection by local coal merchants. The building on the left was the load weighing shed.

Much of the atmosphere of train travel disappeared with the demise of steam and the gradual introduction of more efficient diesel power as this north-bound train is pictured from the down platform in about 1962.

A close-up of the station buildings that shows the access steps leading up to Station Road and on the forecourt is Mr Mike McClure with a new bicycle.

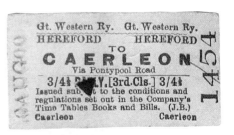

Ready for the off is probably one of the last steam-hauled passenger trains that would have travelled down the eastern valley from Blaenavon through Caerleon to Newport with some fifteen stops on the way during the one-hour journey.

A corner view of the stone-built station buildings with the entrance to the goods yard on the left.

Taken during the 1960s this view is of the footpath access to the station main building entrance and ticket office; situated at Lodge Road just below the road bridge, it provided a useful short cut. In the background can be seen the bridge leading to Ponthir.

Looking east from Station Road bridge is the beginning of part of one of the longest continuous railway line curves in the country. In the middle distance is Penrhos Farm.

Circa 1970 and the demise of Caerleon station is obvious with both platforms and the up line buildings together with the passenger footbridge having been removed. The site had now been sold and converted for use as industrial units.

For railway enthusiasts this is a typical locomotive that was used on the valley lines through Caerleon, a GWR pannier tank engine No. 4639 usually pulling no more than two coaches the loco is adjacent to the footbridge at the up platform in April 1962.

St Cadoc's Children's Home

The ceremony taking place here is the laying of the foundation stone of the Church of England's St. Cadoc's Children's Home in Norman Street on September 14th 1907. The dignitaries in attendance include Alderman Tom Parry, Sir Arthur Mackworth, Lord Tredegar (who had donated the land), The Bishop of Llandaff and Reverend F.W.G. Whitfield M.A. - Vicar of St. Cadoc's Church.

The inscription St Cadoc's Home is set over the main entrance although partly discoloured as the stone was painted for the 1953 Coronation.

The Foundation Stone which is still in-situ adjacent to the front door.
A.M.D.G. from the Latin *'To the greater glory of God'*.

This photograph is from 1935, a period of great economic depression and the need for such places as St. Cadoc's Children's Home was greater than ever. Above is a group of girls at the Home with Miss G.B. Jones (Matron) and Miss C.M. Hughes (Matron's Assistant).

A side view of the house and garden St. Cadoc's Children's Home, the cost of which was met by public subscription. Officially opened in 1908 it was closed in 1965.

Two final pictures from the Home that include an exterior view of the front during the 1960s and a photograph taken in 1938 with staff and children on holiday at Weston-Super-Mare.

Caerleon & District Civic Society sponsored Millennium Wildlife Garden

The Millennium Wildlife Garden (Caerleon's Jewel Amenity) at the start of the project in 2002, it requiring 250 tonnes of fresh top soil due to the poor condition of the existing ground. It was opened in 2005 near the riverside between the Hanbury Arms and the old pumping station. Getting to grips with weeds, Roger Luck wields the strimmer, David Taylor supervises the path construction and Ian Williams operates the dumper truck which was generously loaned free of charge by Peterson Plant Hire of Trostrey.

A welcomed break for the volunteers from Caerleon arts festival preparing the ground for their donated sculpture. Some of their names have been retrieved with apologies to those that have been elusive - Gareth Williams, Tim Davidson, Peter Appleton, Raymond Waller, Andrew Pimblett, David Taylor, Brian Dale, Dr. Russell Rhys.

David Taylor pictured on the left played an important part in the founding of the Millennium Garden project and brought a great deal of enthusiasm and ability. Being a keen gardener himself, he was continually anxious that everything should be 'just right' and used particular skills in knowing exactly whom to approach when 'free of charge assistance' was most needed.

Below is the brass plaque on the commemorative seat.

DAVID EDWIN TAYLOR
1946–2004
TO MARK HIS WORK IN THIS
"MILLENNIUM"
WILDLIFE GARDEN
CAERLEON & DISTRICT CIVIC SOCIETY

Tuesday May 28th 2005 and Caerleon and District Civic Society members are gathered to celebrate the completion and opening of the Wildlife Garden. The site also provides public access to the river view and a bench complete with plaque dedicated to the memory of David Taylor. In the picture left to right are Peter Butler, David Jones, Kim Fisher, Jackie Sully, Carol Jones, Liz Luck, Joshua Sullivan, Jim Sullivan, Alan Stevens, Lyn Nelmes, Hannah Topping, James Taylor (David's son), Norman Stevens, Marie Williams, Barbara Gilfillan, Roger Luck and Carole Stevens.

Norman Stevens (Sponsor and Committee Member) with Liz Luck (Chairperson) sit surrounded by wild flowers that form the scenic and essential habitation for wild life. The sculpture created by Dave Johnson is entitled *'The Eternal Triangle'* - Arthur, Guinevere and Lancelot, the triptich form incorporates traditional Celtic decorations.
(Pictured courtesy of Chris Tinsley, South Wales Argus)

The idea for the garden was started by the residents of Castle Mews and Hanbury Close initiated by Diane and Terry Pearce and a fund was inaugurated in order to save the only accessible open space on the river front from becoming an eyesore or even more probable, was a site for restrictive development of the area. After years of expenditure and legal searching with the co-operation of Newport City Council, the venture was put into the hands of the Caerleon and District Civic Society as an established local representative body to clarify any legal issues. David Taylor was appointed the Society's treasurer and progress chaser. The Green Apple Awards Organisation is part of an international campaign to find environmentally-friendly community projects and give recognition by awards. The presentation of the award to Civic Society representatives took place at the House of Commons in the company of Paul Flynn M.P.

The Ship Inn in 1988 when renovation work was in progress provided a rare opportunity to appreciate the structure as it was originally built during the early part of the nineteenth century. Following the Turnpike Act of 1825 New Road and the toll house were built, linking up with Belmont Hill. Initially the inn occupied the centre section of the building with a dwelling house added at each end and looking to the right, behind the road salt container, a vertical line is visible forming the boundary of the house. To the left are the four windows of a larger house and between them, a bricked-up front doorway.

The pub as it looked in 1991, after the work had been carried out and changed its appearance yet again. Two cars from the past in the picture are a 1960s Humber Sceptre and Ford Sierra.

Lulworth House School at Ultra Pontem as seen in about 1890. The house was built in 1837 in the garden of the White Lion Inn by Mathew Cope, a maltster as his family home. The business adjoining on the left with the lower roofing, was the malt house which had three floors with only six feet headroom. In 1880 the house was used as a Dame School by the daughters Margaret and Martha. Margaret became a well-known singer and married a Mr Alfred Morris who together with Martha ran the school until 1943. It then became the private home of Charles and Vera Lawrence until 1964 when it was sold and converted into the Malthouse Hotel.

A view of the extensive vegetable garden belonging to Lulworth House.

A much later view of Lulworth House as it looked during the 1960s and parked outside is Douglas Burnell Higgs 'Bitza' motor car, a vehicle built along the lines of a 1932 Austin Seven.

September 2000 and there is a new look to the house, it now having been transformed into the Malthouse Hotel with the old malt house building on the left being put into residential use.

Books, Newspapers, Magazines consulted
Bibliography

Guide to Caerleon-on-Usk - W.A. Morris. Lt. Col. RAMC retired. Pub. 1931.

Newport Directories - R.H. Johns 1899, 1908.

Great Western Railway, Ticket Examiners, Current (1928) Fares Book

Caerleon Heritage Trail - Pamphlet published by Caerleon Civic Society, Caerleon Local History Society and Gwent County Council

'Historic Caerleon' A Walk Around - Pamphlet published by Caerleon Civic Society, research by P. Hockey

'Caerleon - Isca' - Roman Legionary Museum Booklet, Pub. 1987, National Museum of Wales

'A Popular Guide to Caerleon' - by ISCA and Atwood Thorne M.B. (Lond.). Pub. 1928. Western Mail Ltd.

South Wales Argus - Various Dates

Souvenir Programme Sat 13th June, 1987 to celebrate the opening of the Roman Legionary Museum

'Hanbury Ale House' - Information Pamphlet 1996.

'Historic Caerleon' - Official Guide of the Urban District Council 1955.

Monmouthshire County Guide 1954 - Pub. Mon. C.C. by the Home Publishing Co., Croydon

The Story of Brynglas House - by D.L. Anne Hobbs, Research by Tony Friend. Pub. by Brynglas Community Educational Centre 1989.

'Steam in South Wales Volume 4' - Monmouthshire by Michael Hale, Pub. Oxford Pub. Co.

History of the Red Cross in Monmouthshire 1920-1918 - by Robin Jones R.G.N., A.I.C.D. Pub. 1988

The Roman Past of Heidenheim and its Twin Towns - by Helmut Weimert. Pub. Heidenheim City Archives 1991

'Newport Transport' 80 Years of Service - E.A. Thomas.

Caerleon Past and Present - Primrose Hockey M.B.E.

Caerleon Endowed Schools 1724-1983 - T.M. Morgan. Pub. Starling Press 1983.

Caerleon Endowed Schools 'The First 270 Years' - T.M. Morgan. Pub. Williams Schools Caerleon

'On The Track of the Caerleon Tramroad - by Kirsten Elliot and Andrew Swift. *'Archive'* Magazine No.32. Published by *'Archive'*, 47-49 High Street, Lydney, Gloucestershire GL15 5DD

'Caerleon Roman Amphitheatre' - by Sir Mortimer Wheeler and Dr. V.E. Nash Williams F.S.A. Pub. by Welsh Office Official Handbook 1970.

'Roman Trail Guide' - by Howard Pell.

'Portraits of the Past' - by Chris Barber and Michael Blackmore. Pub. Blorenge Books.

'Along my Line' - by Gilbert Harding. Pub. Putnam 1953.

Acknowledgements

It is with sincere thanks that I readily give credit to those who generously loaned photographs and ephemera not forgetting their valuable time and knowledge.

Photographs
Valerie Burnell-Jones, Ken Baulch, Mathew Brookner, Leon Bond (Antiques), Rosemary Butler A.M., The Basque Children of '37 Assc. UK, Natalia Benjamin (Oxford), Peter Bevan, Jeffrey Bishop, Peter Butler, Marjorie Bennett (Newport), Tony Bennett (Newport), The late Mrs Marjorie Coopey, Geofrey Crew (Newport), Lynne Daniels, Peta Davies née Coopey (Cardiff), Alice Eddolls, Valerie Eason née Shierson, Jill Edwards, Tony and Maureen Friend (Newport Historian), Kim Fisher, Wendy Flindell (Newport), Sonia Fisher née Phillips (Langstone), Derek Gear, Royce and the late Marion Gardener MBE, Martin and Kathleen Green, Elsie Gibbens, Ken Graham, Frank Harding BA, BEd. (Cwmbran), Martyn Hazell, David Hall (Ponthir), Sue Hughes, Glamorgan and Gwent Archeological Trust, Godfrey 'Toshy' Hill, David Hawke (Ponthir), Roger Harris, Ian Irving (Ultra Pontem), The late Margaret Jones, Douglas Morgan-Jones, James Kirkwood MBE, FRSA, Cliff Knight (Newport Historian), Raymond and Kath Llewelyn, Joyce Mapp, Nigel Miggins (Ultra Pontem), Lynette Morris, Gordon Murray, Heather Morgan, Ron Morgan, Ann and Terry Maloney, Canon Rev. Philip R.S. Morgan TD, MA, Adelaide Morgan, Pauline O'Sullivan, Jim Povall, Catherine Philpott, Connie and Russell Powell, The late Clive Powell, Ken Rees, Kath Rushton, Dr. Russel and Gillian Rees (Ffwrwm), Joyce Richards (Hanbury Garage), Ifor Thom, Mark and Margaret Thom, Lionel Turner, Bob Trett, Terry Underwood (Author, Historian and Playwright), Henry West, Stephen Wilmot (Llantrissant), T. Ward, William Howard Wookey, William J. Wookey, Nigel Young (Caerleon Website www. Caerleon.net).

Time, Advice, Information and Useful Assistance
Clive Bourne, Simon Boyle (Lord Lt. of Gwent, C. St. John), Mike Buckingham (Reporter, Columnist South Wales Argus), Stephen and Eryl Benavente, Spencer and Sheila Basford (Postmaster), Douglas and Beryl Burnell-Higgs, A. Cox, Roger Cucksey (Keeper of Fine Art, Newport City), Michael Cook (Hanbury Arms), Marilyn Custard, Ann Collings-Vicary (Librarian St. Cadoc's Hospital), John Cooke (Foreman retired Pattison Eurotech Ltd.), Janet Davies (Caerleon AFC), Malgwyn Davies (Order of St. John), Allan Dowling (Caldicot), Simon Derrett, Ray Davies (Caerphilly Council), Ron V. Drake (Newport), Canon Arthur Edwards, Austin and Jean Evans, Margaret Ellis (Legion Museum), O. Evans, Simon Ford (Pattison Eurotech), Enrique Garay, Gail Giles BSc., Paul Harris, Miriam Hando (Newport), Ron Jones (Caerleon Golf Club), Carol Jones (Ponthir), Leslie Knight (Newport Council), Wendy Lewis (Caerphilly), Stephen Llewellyn, Elizabeth and Jill Marcusson, Kathleen Morgan, Geoff Nicolle (Haverfordwest), Irene Phillis (Newport), Florence Pritchard (Newport - a former Caerleon resident), Phil Rollings, Lyn Richards, William Roberts, Jackie Stokes (Autistic Society), Jeff Snook, Tina Snook (Ponthir), Sandra Spiteri, Denvil and Gillian Stamp (Ross on Wye), Miguel Santiago (Priory Hotel), Douglas Slater (Newport), Graham Smith (Senior Ambulance Officer Retd.).

Sincere thanks also to Canon Arthur Edwards for his kind foreword and to Malcolm Thomas and staff of Old Bakehouse Publications for their helpful and encouraging support.

Previous publications by Norman Stevens -

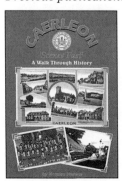